LIFE IN THE FAST LANE
Two Tomcats Strike it Lucky!

SONDRA BURCHFIELD

"Life in the Fast Lane - Two Tomcats Strike it Lucky!," by Sondra Burchfield. ISBN 978-1-60264-600-1.

Published 2010 by Virtualbookworm.com Publishing Inc., P.O. Box 9949, College Station, TX 77842, US. ©2010, Sondra Burchfield. All rights reserved. No part of this publication may be reproduced, stored in a retrieval system, or transmitted in any form or by any means, electronic, mechanical, recording or otherwise, without the prior written permission of Sondra Burchfield.

Manufactured in the United States of America.

Table of Contents

Introduction

My friends made me write this book. They think driving back and forth across the country each summer with two tom cats is a hilarious experience, especially since they are not the ones doing it!

On paper, my husband and I appear to have lived a fairly normal, somewhat successful life. We have been married 45 years and are from the same small town in Iowa. We spent most of our professional lives living in downtown Chicago.

My husband, John, spent his career as a corporate attorney and later as vice president of several corporations. I started my career as a high school history teacher. I later became a senior editor with the textbook division of Doubleday and Company, was a member of the training staff of The Great Books Foundation, and ended my career as a counselor at a small liberal arts college.

Since the third year of our marriage we have had a cat as a pet. It has just been since our retirement, however, that it may appear cats have taken over our lives!

As a retired couple we now live in Southern California in the winter and on a lake near the Iowa/Minnesota border in the summer. We currently have two tom cats we recently adopted from a local Humane Society that are a part of our family. The tom cats do not like one another, however, they travel by car with us between our two homes. It's not a "fun" trip for us or the cats!

My husband and I are both "type A" personalities so we make "tracks" to get to our destination as soon as possible. We often drive at speeds in excess of the speed limit. While our two tom cats may not think "living in the fast lane" is much fun, they have done quite well considering their origins.

Finally, the stories that follow are true accounts of the antics of our recently adopted tom cats. I didn't make anything up!

LESSON ONE
NEVER ADOPT TWO ADULT TOM CATS

Hi! My name is Max. I'm a very handsome five-year old male yellow tabby--a domestic short hair is my official pedigree. I'm a very loving cat who likes to be petted, and, in return, I'll lick your hand.

I had an awful thing happen to me though. I had a wonderful mistress who was very kind to me, but then her boyfriend moved into our house. He was mean to me. Every time I tried to jump on his lap, he would push me away. I always slept on my mistress' feet, but he would throw me off the bed. One day my mistress told me we were going to go for a car ride. (I don't like car rides, especially if we are going to the bad veterinarian who took out my front claws.)

This car ride was the worst of my life. My mistress took me to the local Humane Society and told the staff she could no longer keep me. I'm sure that bad boyfriend put her up to this. I think there is something wrong with people who do not like animals.

After my mistress left, I was put in a cage. There were many other cats in cages. By the way, I do not like other cats. I started crying and crying, but nobody seemed to care about me. I was lonely, afraid, and heartbroken.

I lived in this awful cage for about one month when this loud-talking man walked in one day and started looking at all the cats in cages. When he came to my cage, he stuck his hand through the mesh to pet me and then I licked his hand. He said something like I seemed like a nice cat and he would be back to see me some more. I was so depressed, though, because I didn't think he would ever return. By now, I had figured out that some cats got to leave their cages because they got adopted.

Well, guess what? The next day the loud talking man returned and had his wife with him. She took me out of the cage and petted me and I, of course, licked her hand too. I think she was quite impressed with me because after about one hour the loud talking man and his wife got me out of my cage and put me in their driving machine.

At this point I was quite scared because I wasn't sure if I got to go to their home. I was shaking quite a bit during the short ride, but I didn't do anything wrong like accidently poop or anything. (Sometimes if I get real scared, I poop!)

Pretty soon we arrived at a large building on West Lake Okoboji. I think the building is called a condominium. At any rate, the loud talking man carried me inside their condo and told me this was my new home. I didn't know whether to trust him or not so I found the litter box as soon as possible and hid in it. They didn't bother me. They just let me be.

After about an hour, I felt less scared and decided to move slowly out of the litter box and explore. Pretty soon I came upon a beautiful cat bed. Since I was exhausted from the trauma of the day, I crawled into the bed and went to sleep. A couple of hours later, the nice lady gave me some delicious cat food. Oh boy, I thought, maybe I really have been adopted, and this is my new home.

When night came, the nice lady put me in her bed and petted me. After a while I jumped over to the loud talking man's bed and then he petted me. Yipppeee, I thought, I really have been adopted. I decided to name my new owners Master Loud Talker and Mistress Nicey.

After about one month of a wonderful new life living on West Lake Okoboji, Master and Mistress started packing a lot of boxes. I started to worry that they might move away and abandon me. Well, one day Master carried me to his white driving machine and locked me inside. I saw all my basic needs (my bed, food, water, and my litter box). Pretty soon Master and Mistress got in the white machine and Mistress Nicey started driving. I got in my bed, but I was a nervous wreck. After about 30 minutes, Mistress Nicey pulled onto this large road called an interstate highway. Master told her to "hit it!" She started driving real fast. I got even more scared and started shaking even more. All of a sudden I let out a big poop!

Master said some bad words. Mistress Nicey pulled off the road and took my cat bed outside and cleaned it with baking soda. I hid in the litter box. I kept trying to tell them how sorry I was, but I don't think they understood. Well, at any rate, for the duration of a very tiring three day trip I never left my litter box except when they carried me into one of those awful motel rooms where I was even more scared and hid under the bed.

2

After three days of being cooped up in the frightening white machine, we stopped and Master said we were home. I didn't understand. Do they have two homes? Master carried me inside and you wouldn't believe what I saw. If this place was my new home, I'd never seen anything so large. There were long halls where I could get up a big run. There were all kinds of fun places to explore. It didn't take me long to feel at home here because they brought all of my "stuff" and put it in place!

The best part of MY NEW HOME is there's a swimming pool on the back patio, and I am allowed to drink from it! All in all life was now wonderful for me. I had the whole place to myself, I got great food, and I got to sleep wherever I wanted, even on Mistress Nicey's feet!

MY WORST NIGHTMARE!

Things were going along wonderfully until one day Master and Mistress went for a drive and when they came back, they wouldn't let me in Master Loud Talker's office. All of a sudden I started hearing a goat baying in there. I was scared to death. I thought: "Oh, my God, they brought home a goat to live with us!"

Pretty soon the goat started clawing the carpet by the door. I wondered if maybe it wasn't a goat. I don't think goats claw carpeting. Whatever the animal was it started baying louder and louder and clawing and clawing and making a terrible racket. Finally, Mistress Nicey opened the door.

It was my most dreaded nightmare! It was an all-white cat like Queenie. You see, the reason that my Master and Mistress got me was because their beloved Queenie had died.

I couldn't think of anything to do but attack this intruder cat. I jumped right at it and bit half of one ear off. Blood was everywhere. Mistress Nicey yelled and yelled at me.

Mistress Nicey had to rush the white intruder to the veterinarian. I guess it cost about $1,000 to get that stupid cat's ear sewed back together. I didn't feel any remorse, though. I was not about to let a new cat take my place as head of the household. I vowed to show that new cat who was going to be the boss.

When the new cat returned with its ear all bandaged, I had a very firm talk with him. I said: "Listen you cross-eyed intruder, I'm going to make your life miserable. Don't you ever get on Master or Mistress' lap or I'll kill you! Do you understand me?"

"Yes, I don't want to be a problem. I'm a very gentle boy, and I don't like to fight. Please don't hurt me again."

"Are you gay or something? You look like a girl. Too bad you're cross-eyed."

I'm not cross-eyed. I have one blue eye and one green eye which is very distinctive. This abnormality occurs in humans as well and is called heterochromia iridis which means different colors of the iris.

Shut up, Cross-eyes and don't use big words with me. I'm a macho man—not a phony prissy cat like you! Are you sure you're not gay?

I don't think so, but I am a gentleman, and I might add you are not!

That's it! I'm going to bite your other ear off. Oh, shucks, Mistress Nicey intervened. See, you already are getting me in trouble. I will find a way to get rid of you.

By the way, how come you have an infection in your eye and are so skinny?

Well, I think my first owner died and her neighbors let me stay on their property, but not inside the house. I'm an indoor cat so I was very frightened. I took off exploring trying to find my mistress, but I guess I just got lost. One day a nice man found me all huddled under a porch, and he took me to the local humane society where I was put in a cage in the infirmary and put on some medicine. That's when Mistress Nicey found me. Even though I looked terrible at the time, Mistress Nicey said I was a gentle cat and she would adopt me. Master wasn't that thrilled. He told Mistress Nicey that there were other prettier white cats out front in other cages.

Mistress Nicey, I guess, was determined to adopt me. She thought I looked like her cat, Queenie, so I got lucky except for you "Jerkface!"

You ever call me that again, I will bite off your other ear.

Okay, I'm sorry. I won't hurt your feelings again.

What's your name, by the way?

Mistress Nicey is calling me Snowball. It's not my real name, but I don't know how to let her know what my real name is so I guess that's what my new name is. Sometimes, though, Mistress and Master slip and call me Queenie.

Oh, brother. How am I going to compete with that?

I've got to find a plan to get rid of Snowball. I know—I'll attack him at night when Master and Mistress are asleep. My plan isn't working too well. Whenever I attack Snowball at night, even though she seems to be sleeping, Mistress Nicey shoots me with a terrorizing water gun.

I know. I'll wait until Snowball leaves the bedroom. Oh, boy, there he goes out of the bedroom. Where is that stupid cross-eyed cat? Can't find him anywhere. Ah Ha! He's hiding under the lid of the grand piano. I'm afraid to jump up in there. One thing I'll say for that stupid cat, he knows how to find good hiding places. This whole situation is exhausting me!

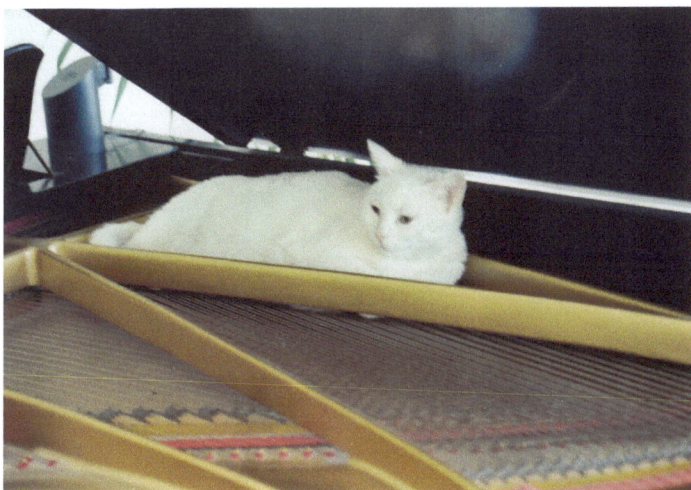

To escape from Max, Snowball found unique hiding places such as under the lid of the grand piano!

MOST CATS DO NOT LIKE TO RIDE IN CARS!

MAX AND SNOWBALL'S FIRST ROAD TRIP TOGETHER –JUNE, 2007

Ohhhhh Nooooo -- the dreaded white machine! (Master calls it a Mercedes ML -- what ever that means.) I've got to escape. Oh, no – I'm locked in the white machine and there's "Fatso" Snowball. I can't stand that cat! Mistress Nicey always calls Snowball a beautiful boy. The truth is Snowball is ugly. First, he has one blue eye and one green eye so he looks cross-eyed. Second, he's an old codger –at least eight years old. Did you ever see a cat with a wrinkled forehead? Third, since moving into MY house he has become obese. He's so fat he can hardly walk. I, on the other hand, am a handsome cat. Master says I am. Further, Snowball is stupid! Master even thinks he's stupid—calls him a troglodyte.

I need to do something drastic to see if Master and Mistress will turn the white machine around and take me back home. I'm going to let out my most harrowing MEOWS. Can you believe they're laughing at me? Snowball just sits there like a dumb bell—doesn't make a sound.

Well, looks like I'm stuck in the white machine. Oh, God, there's that puny litter box they make us use on road trips. At least it's got a cover on it so I can hide in it. I see my bed. Maybe I should take a big poop in my bed and then Master and Mistress might turn the white machine around. I did this on my first trip with them, but they didn't turn around so guess I won't try it yet.

I just heard Master tell Mistress Nicey to "hit it!" As I recall that means keep the white machine going over the speed limit. This is when I get really dizzy.

DAY ONE - ALBUQUERQUE OR BUST!

I've been cooped up in the white machine for 12 hours. I'm suffering from nervous exhaustion—hid in the litter box all day. Fatso Snowball slept in his bed all day.

I think we're in the middle of "fly over" country!

Uh Oh! It looks like we're staying in one of those awful motels. Master is going to carry me to the room, and Mistress Nicey, of course, will carry "Fatso!"

Master tells me we are going to ride in an elevator. We're in this huge metal box and the doors slam shut. I think we're in a GAS CHAMBER! I can't stop shaking. If these doors ever open, I'm going to jump out of Master's arms and run. Here's my chance—I'm out of here. Master is yelling at me and calling me bad names! I see an open room with an ice machine. Mistress Nicey is in "hot" pursuit of me. She grabs me by the tail just before I was going to jump down an open drain pipe hole. She's calling me a s… ….!

Captured again and I'm in this awful motel room. I'm desperate—no place to hide under the beds. Wait . . . there's a small space under the headboard I can squeeze into. They'll never find me there. I'm not coming out of my hiding place even to eat.

I think they're asleep now. I'll creep out and grab a little snack.

It must be morning. They're both up and looking for me. Oh, no -- the terrorizing water gun! Master Loud Talker shoots me. Mistress Nicey grabs me and back I go into the dreaded white machine.

7

I'm going to catch a bird and put it right on this blue and white cushion. Mistress will love it!

DAY TWO - CAN'T WAIT TO SEE GREENSBURG, KANSAS

Today was another terrorizing day of moving fast in the white machine. I'm not moving out of this litter box. When we stop for gas, Fatso Snowball gets up on his hind legs and looks out the window. I hope someone sees him and kidnaps him.

Oh! Oh! The white machine is getting stopped by the police. This seems to happen frequently on our road trips. Master usually says some bad words when this happens, but he's not this time. The police tell Master and Mistress they have to detour around Greensburg, Kansas, because of all the tornado destruction. "Fatso" again is standing on his hind legs looking out the window—tells me he sees rows of semi trucks carting debris and uprooted trees away.

Spent ten hours in the white machine, and we're staying in another one of those awful motels. We got to park right in front of our room this time so I didn't shake too much when they put me in the room. No place to hide, but I'm not quite as nervous as yesterday when we had to ride in the gas chamber to get to our room.

8

DAY THREE -- LET ME OUT OF HERE!

Oh, God, another day locked in the white machine so I have to hide again in the litter box. After about eight hours, I start smelling something familiar. We've stopped. I slowly move out of the litter box. Yippee!!!!!!!!!! It's the lake where I was born!

Oh, boy, I love this place. I get to go out on the grass here. In the Southern California, I get shot with the water gun if I leave the patio—something about "coyote watch!"

I know what I'm going to do this year. I'm going to catch a bird and present it to Mistress Nicey. Then she'll see I'm her favorite cat! I'll bring my catch right to the porch door. No, better idea—I'll put my catch on one of her favorite blue and white-stripped porch cushions. She'll love that!

MAX AND SNOWBALL'S FIRST SUMMER TOGETHER AT THE LAKE

Now, listen, Fatso Snowball this is our summer place. It's small so we might have to share some space occasionally, but I have certain rules you have to follow. You are not allowed to sleep on either twin bed when Master and Mistress are in the beds. Only I get to sleep with Master and Mistress. Do you understand?

Boo Hoo! Boo Hoo!

Oh, God, now you're turning into a cry baby!

Well, how do you think I feel? I lost my first mistress too. I feel lonely and lost. I need affection sometimes. I just want to fit into my new family and be a part of it. You're so mean to me. Wasn't I nice to you Max when you were frightened riding in the driving machine?

Well, okay, but you only can sleep at the foot of the bed.

There's a nice window seat in the bedroom you can sleep on also, and you can watch outside for rabbits and squirrels. However, during the daytime I get to sleep on the window seat and patrol for rabbits and squirrels. I plan to kill one of those "suckers" this year.

You better not do that, you know. Remember, you don't have any claws and you might get some sort of disease from biting one of those little animals. I think they're cute. Why don't you just leave them alone?

Shut up Fatso. I'll do what I want.

Hey, Jerkface Max, why are you drinking from that glass candle stick holder?

Boy, are you dumb! I drink from it because the water is cooler than the water in our water bowl.

Could I drink from it too?

I suppose, but don't knock it over or it will break.

Oh, dear I've broken the glass candlestick holder. Mistress Nicey might get mad at me. I'm so sorry.

The reason you broke it is because you're so fat you can't move sleekly like me. Now we have to go back to drinking water from that stupid bowl.

Ha! Ha! Ha! Mistress Nicey didn't get mad at me. See what she did. She put a plastic martini glass right where the glass candle stick holder was so we can both drink from it! Oh, boy, you're right, the water is much cooler than from out of our drinking bowl. This is just totally cool. I hope we get to have this martini glass with us when we go back to California.

Okay, Fatso, now I've got a project that I need your help on. When Master and Mistress go to sleep tonight, I'm going to start biting through the screen door and make a hole in it so I can go out and catch me a rabbit or a squirrel. Would you help with your claws?

Sure I will, but Master and Mistress might get mad at us.

Don't worry. They're suckers for us. They'll think it's a cute idea!

Hey, man, we've made a big enough hole so I can squeeze through it.

10

I'm outside all by myself.

Oh, Oh, Master just got up and he's coming out on the porch. You better get back in here Max!

Oh, Oh, Master has just seen the hole in the screen and you're outside. He's saying lots of BAD WORDS! Says he's going to the hardware store and get a new screen. Mistress Nicey is building a barricade of books to cover the hole in the screen.

Master and Mistress spent all morning installing the new screen. I don't think you better try to make a hole in the new screen or they'll really get mad at us.

We're going to do it again tonight and you're going to help me. It's totally cool being outside without Master and Mistress patrolling us.

Okay, they're asleep. Let's get to work.

This is hard work Max. I'm exhausted.

Shut up and keep working. We're through. I'm out of here!

I'm going to go hide so Master and Mistress won't think I'm a bad cat. You better get back inside. It's morning and they'll find you outside.

I just heard Master say more BAD WORDS—something about getting the thickest screen he can buy!

Again, Master and Mistress spent all morning installing a second, thicker screen. Max, I'm not going to help you tonight. And, anyway, I don't think we can bite or claw our way through this screen.

I suppose you're right Fatso, but you have to admit we had fun with this project!

MAX AND SNOWBALL'S RETURN TRIP TO CALIFORNIA -- SEPTEMBER, 2007

DAY ONE – CAN'T GET OUT OF DODGE FAST ENOUGH!

Oh, no, here we go again in the white driving machine. I think we're headed back to California. Max still won't get out of the litter box. During the first 45 minutes of our trek, three unpleasant events occurred. First, Max pooped in the litter box. (His poop really stinks!) Second, I had to poop real badly, so I meowed loudly at Max to get out of the litter box. I took a poop too. In general, the car really stunk! In an attempt to prevent asphyxiation, Master poured "massive" amounts of baking soda into the litter box. In addition, he was saying a lot of bad words. Third, Mistress Nicey got pulled over by the highway patrol for speeding 85 mph in a 65 mph zone. Again, Master was saying bad words: "How in the . . . . . . could you be driving 85 mph?" Mistress reminded him of his two "pullovers" for exceeding the speed limit and that shut him up!

The patrolman asked Mistress to explain why she had a California license and an Iowa license plate. She told him we lived at the Lake for six months per year (big lie), but that this year we were returning to California early because Master was scheduled for surgery (true). The patrolman then asked Mistress if we were just beginning our trip and asked if the two cats traveled the entire way with us. Mistress told him we were just starting our trip and that regrettably the cats did travel all the way with us. He laughed! Mistress didn't get a ticket!

Made it to Dodge City, Kansas, (600 mile drive) the first night and stayed in a semi-dumpy motel. Horror of horrors—the bed frames did not go all the way to the floor. This is a bad situation for people traveling with cats. Naturally, Max, who is such a coward, would not be coaxed from underneath the bed the next morning. Took Master and Mistress 20 minutes to route him out! I, of course, was waiting by the door to go. I never want to be left behind.

DAY TWO -- A BETTER MOTEL BUT A "KILLER" DRIVE!

We made it to Holbrook, Arizona, the second night (750 miles). Max spent the entire day riding in the litter box!

We stayed at a nice motel where the bed frames reached the floor. However, the next morning Master and Mistress could not find Max. They could see no place where he could hide except behind the dresser and he wasn't there. Finally, Master opened one of the drawers in the dresser and there was Max—shaking like a leaf!

12

DAY THREE -- HOME AT LAST BUT ARE WE HAPPY?

Again, Max spent the final travel day in the litter box. Made it home by 2 p.m. only to discover we had no air conditioning. The outside temperature was 105 degrees. A repairman arrived the next day and made Master pay $760 so we could have air conditioning!

Master and Mistress seem quite pleased that Max and I are getting along better. I heard them say: "Max and Snowball seem to have reached a relationship similar to disdainful détente—like a lot of marriages!"

MAX AND SNOWBALL'S TRIP TO THE LAKE --JUNE, 2008

DAY ONE – DOESN'T LOOK LIKE WE'LL MAKE ALBUR-QUERE TONIGHT!

HA HA HA HA HA HA! You're so stupid, Max! I knew Master and Mistress were going to trick you into believing today would just be another normal day in the household. I knew by the way Mistress was running around the house at 4 a.m. drawing blinds and such that we were going on another one of their trips.

You didn't have a clue until Master picked you up and "dumped" you into the car. I was waiting by the door to go. I love to travel!

Oh, cool. They have a nice pet taxi with a soft cushion inside. I'm going to stretch out in there. Another sign you are stupid Max -- you always ride in the litter box.

Gee, I wonder if Mistress remembered to pack the cat suitcase with our plastic martini glass. I love to drink my water from a martini glass because I have a very large stomach so I don't have to bend over so far.

Oh, noooooo! You did it again! Pooped before we are a mile out of town. It stinks in here! Master and Mistress are arguing about whether to stop and scoop the poop or carry on. Since Mistress is driving, she stops to scoop out the poop! Master is saying some BAD WORDS!

Max, you are so low class. Why can't you learn to control your bodily functions? Shut up "Fatso!" I'm shaking so badly I can't control anything! Haven't you ever heard the expression "scared shitless?"

Snowball tries to comfort Max by curling up just outside the litter box—Max's secure place to ride while traveling!

After about five hours as we are heading up the mountain road toward Flagstaff, Arizona, we come to a huge traffic jam. People are outside of their cars talking with one another. Some people say there's been a bad accident ahead and the road needs to be cleared. After about one hour, we start moving again. It was a bad accident. A semi jack-knifed across the freeway.

Master and Mistress don't think we can make it to Albuquerque tonight because they have lost so much travel time. Albuquerque is always their goal because there are three La Quinta Inns there that welcome pets.

Man, this has been one long day (13 ½ hours on the road), but we finally make Albuquerque and stay in a La Quinta Inn. The bed frames go all the way to the floor so Max can't hide under the bed.

Hey, Max, Mistress Nicey remembered to bring our martini glass!

DAY TWO -- TORNADO ALLEY -- HERE WE COME!

We're up at 5 a.m. because Master and Mistress want to "hit the road" early. We're taking a new route this year. We're going to go north on

14

Interstate 25 to Colorado Springs and then cut over to Interstate 70 across Kansas (Tornado Alley).

Oh, God "Fatso" I don't know how much longer I can take of this riding in the "white machine." It's okay, Max. I'll lie down in front of the litter box so you'll feel more secure. Thanks, "Fatso!"

See, things are going along quite well. I think I'm going to get back on the cushion in the pet taxi -- a lot more comfortable – and take a nap. Max, what in God's name are you doing?

I want to try out the pet taxi too. You've got your butt right in my face. Oh, Oh, Mistress Nicey just snapped a photo of us together in the pet taxi, but only your butt is showing. I bet she'll show that photo to her friends -- like they care!

It's been another long day (11 hours) so this route is longer than our "old" route -- bet we won't go this way again. Master is checking us into a motel.

A woman is coming over to the car. I'm getting back in the litter box. I'm scared. Snowball, are you stupid or what? You're standing on your hind legs looking out the window. That woman might try to kidnap you.

No she won't. Mistress Nicey is in the car and will protect me.

"What a beautiful cat! She has such gorgeous eyes!"

HA HA HA HA HA HA! That lady called you a girl! I always knew you were a "girlie" boy dressed in drag!

Oh, Oh! The bed frames in this motel room don't go to the floor!

DAY THREE – THE LAKE AT LAST – THANK GOD ALMIGHTY – THE LAKE AT LAST!

Max, quit being such a coward! Get out from underneath the bed. Master and Mistress want to "roll!" Oh, Oh, here comes the water gun with vinegar and water. I'm just going to wait at the door. They're really spraying you. You're going to be sopping wet and stink like vinegar. You look like a drowned rat and you stink too!

15

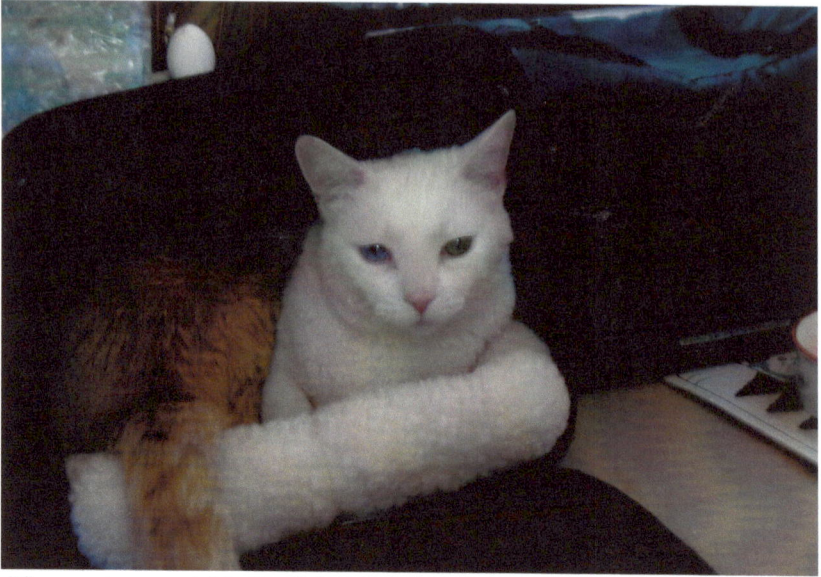

Max ventures outside the litter box and tries to squeeze inside the pet taxi where Snowball is resting!

I'm not going to leave the litter box today.

Good!

After about nine hours, Mistress Nicey starts talking her "cat" talk to us. Says something about we're at the "lakie wakie! Fatso, get up on your hind legs and see if you recognize where we are.

We are at the lake! Oh, boy, this is a fun place, and we don't have to worry about coyotes here!

The condo looks just the same, but there are about six boxes in the living room. Master and Mistress start opening the boxes and putting things away.

Let's take a long nap, Max. I don't think we're going anywhere tomorrow.

DAY FOUR – FIRST DAY AT THE LAKE!

Master is trying to build something. He's out in the hallway, and he's saying A LOT OF BAD WORDS – something about don't ever order

Naps are good!

anything again that says: "SOME ASSEMBLY REQUIRED!" With the help of his neighbor, Master finishes his building project, and he's bringing it inside the condo.

Hey, Max -- come here and look. It's a really cool white window seat with a bright lime green cushion. It's got cupboards in the bottom we can hide in!

SNOWBALL AND MAX'S RETURN ROAD TRIP TO CALIFORNIA - SEPTEMBER, 2008

I am an excellent traveler. Mistress thinks my former owner was either a truck driver or a couple who owned a mobile home. Max hates to travel, shakes the whole time, and refuses to get out of the litter box.

This was my second summer to go to Lake Okoboji, and boy, did I have a ball this summer! One day early this summer Mistress Nicey left the porch to go inside for a minute so I took off exploring. (I like to explore, and Mistress thinks my first owner couldn't find me because I had taken off exploring.) Well, at any rate, I went to the edge of the front lawn and came to a very high break wall. Beneath was a sand beach. I thought it would be fun to roll in the sand so I jumped off the wall and rolled and rolled on the sand.

I was having a ball until Mistress Nicey found me and shot me with the water gun which contained vinegar and water. Even so, I continued to jump off that wall all summer and continued to get squirted with the water gun. It was worth it though!

Max kept bragging he was going to catch a bird for Mistress Nicey and present it to the porch door. He's such a jerk! He mainly caught flying leaves in his mouth and put them by the porch door. One day, though, he did catch a baby mouse and took it to the porch door. Mistress Nicey "freaked out" and called Master to throw the mouse in the Lake.

DAY ONE – YOU NEED TO BE ON DRUGS TO DRIVE ACROSS NEBRASKA

As we were leaving the Lake condo, Max hid under the bed so Mistress had to shoot off the water gun with vinegar and water. The bedroom really smelled bad. As soon as Max was put in the car, he immediately got in the litter box. About 15 minutes into our trip, Max let out a big poop. Boy, did it smell! Further, he got out of the litter box and started whining and whining. Mistress pulled over and scooped the poop out. Boy, was I glad because the whole car smelled! As soon as Mistress scooped out the poop, Max got back into the litter box. During this time Master was saying a lot of bad words!

We made it to the western edge of Nebraska the first night. It's a long way across Nebraska. Someone wrote a sign on a gas station bathroom door that said: "You have to be on drugs to drive across Nebraska!"

Max didn't get into too much trouble in the motel room because the only place he could find to hide was behind the television credenza. Lucky for Master and Mistress the bottom of the credenza had drawers so all they had to do was remove a drawer and pull Max out.

DAY TWO – WE WON'T BE TAKING THIS ROUTE AGAIN!

Before we left the Lake this year, Master said he wanted to take the northern route (through Colorado, Utah, and Nevada) home. He said he was sick of driving through "cowboy" country (through western Kansas, Oklahoma, and Texas).

Driving through the mountains in Colorado at 80 mph made Max dizzier

18

than usual. He started to act like he was going to throw up.

"Oh, God, Max, don't throw up!"

"Shut up, Fatso. I told you I can't control my bodily functions when I'm riding in a car.

We lucked out—Max didn't throw up. Further, about half way through the mountains Master said we wouldn't be taking this route again because it's too hard to drive. Mistress Nicey agreed!

We made it to Interstate 15 in southern Utah and stayed for the night. Max didn't get into any trouble in the motel this time!

DAY THREE – LIFE IN THE FAST LANE!

We were on the road early the next morning and heading for Las Vegas when Mistress Nicey and Master had a BIG argument. It seems Master wanted to cut two hours off our trip home by taking a route a friend had told him about. This route would cut through "raw" desert, and there would be no services for two hours. Mistress yelled: "I'm not cutting through "raw" desert in 112 degree heat with no services for two hours!" Master yelled back: "You won't try anything new!"

Finally, a compromise was reached. Mistress Nicey promised to go the friend's route in October when they planned to drive to Las Vegas to see Tony Bennett.

As Mistress Nicey pulled onto Interstate 10 in California, cars were speeding around her. Master asked her how fast she was going. She said she was going 80 mph. Master said: "Step on it. This is California. We're in the fast lane now!"

LESSON THREE
TAKING PHOTOGRAPHS OF CATS CAN BE DIFFICULT!

Master and Mistress are very nice to us except at Christmas time when they insist on making us miserable by posing for "stupid" cat photos which they then make into their annual Christmas cards. They told us they have done this for the past 15 years. They got the idea from a "Saturday Night Live" skit called "Toones, the Cat." Toones was a dead stuffed cat driving a car down a mountainous road. As the car careens down the mountain road, a celebrity sits in the passenger seat and chats with Toones. At the end of the skit, Toones careens off the mountain road and crashes only to return the next week – I guess because cats have nine lives!

Master and Mistress thought that skit was very funny so they decided to try to get their cats to do non-cat-like things for their Christmas cards in the hope their friends would find the cards humorous. Well, evidently, their friends think the cards are a riot, so I guess we're going to have to get photographed each year at Christmas.

Last year, however, their attempt to photograph us on their boat almost ended in disaster. Mistress Nicey wrote the following e-mail to her friends about what happened:

"During an attempted Christmas card cat photo shoot on the Burchfield boat, "Summertime," Max, the cowardly tom cat, went missing. He had been under the negligent "watch" of John who was driving the boat. Neither the photographer, an enlisted neighbor who was stationed on the dock, or Sonnie, who was stationed on the bow of the boat with Snowball, saw where Max went.

After an extensive search of the boat, including the engine compartment, Sonnie took Snowball back to the condo and instructed John to go back out in the Lake and look for Max. As Sonnie approached the condo porch, she saw Max at the condo door shaking like a leaf and looking like a drowned rat!

Max had jumped off the boat stern, had swum ashore, had climbed over rocks and a 25 foot bank, and had "high tailed" it to the condo porch!

20

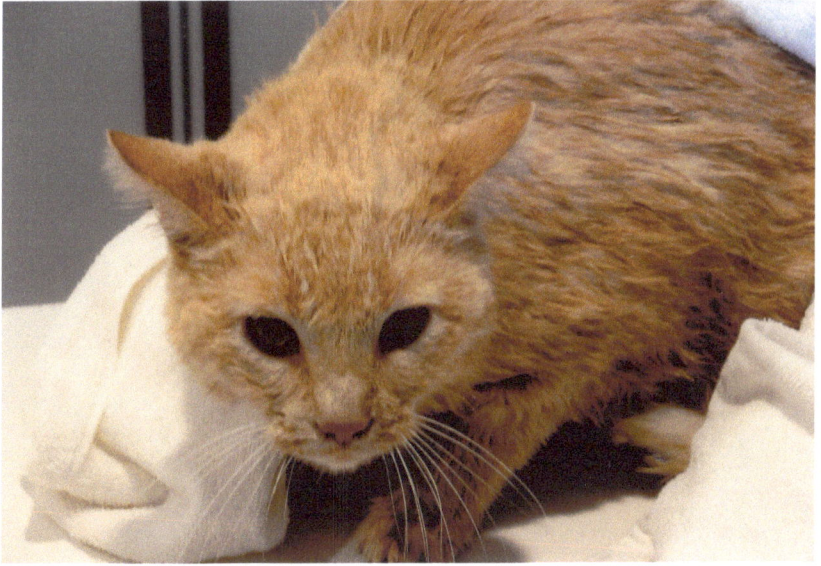

Michael Phelps, I'm not!

It is reported there will be no further attempts to photograph the cats on the boat."

That was last year. They're already starting to talk about next year's idea – something about the swimming pool. It doesn't sound good for us!

Cats Star in Christmas Cards Past!

Warmest Greetings!

Who's going to drive the boat while we water ski?

Captain Bill Maas takes "Queenie" for a ride on "The Queen!"

Mistress Nicey was on the Iowa Great Lakes Maritime Museum Board when the Board led the fund drive to save the old amusement park at the Lake from a developer who was going to tear down the amusement park and build condos. The Board needed to raise $5.5 million dollars in 41 days! The Board raised $7.2 million and saved the Park! Queenie celebrated by going for a ride on the Park's tour boat, The Queen!

I'm way up here because I think the Captain might let me steer the boat!

Happy Holidays

Sonnie and John Burchfield
Queenie Too

"How long do you think it took them to get me to look like I'm driving the golf cart?"

It is good to be Queen!
One of Mistress Nicey's friends made the crown for me!

Happy Holidays

Safe Cruisin'
in '03
The Burchfields
Queenie Too!

I love to sunbathe, especially on the boat!

"Hasta La Vista Baby!"

Happy Holidays

Sonnie and John Burchfield
Queenie Too

As our newly elected Governor Arnold Schwarzenegger would say:
"Hasta La Vista, Baby!"

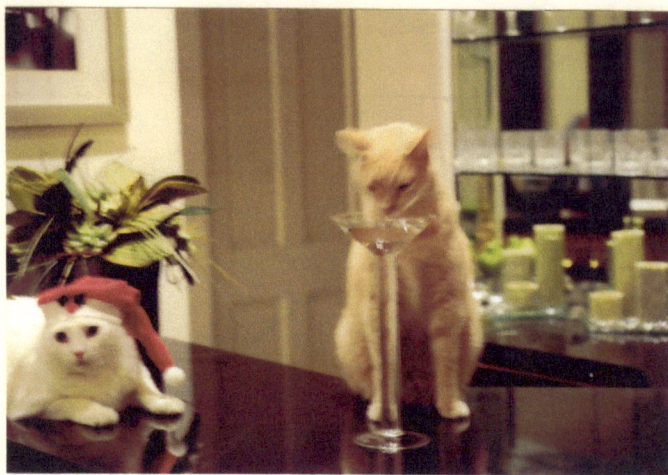

A little drier with an olive, please!

happy
holidays
2007

It is good to have a
friend! Sonnie and
John-Snowball & Max too!

They pulled a fast one on me - slipped the stupid Santa Claus hat
on me while I was napping!

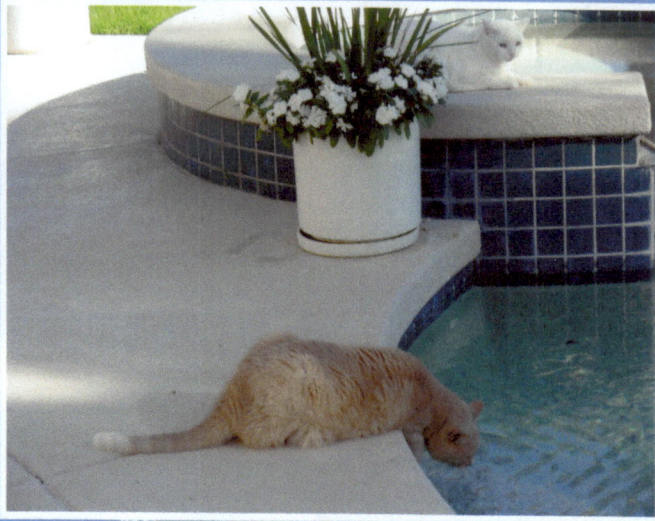

Our portfolio is down so
we're drinking a lot!
Max and Snowball
Sonnie and John too!

wishing you *happy holidays*

Max, you shouldn't drink out of the pool. It makes you throw up!

www.ingramcontent.com/pod-product-compliance
Lightning Source LLC
Chambersburg PA
CBHW041803040426
42448CB00001B/29